LET THERE BE LIGHT

Titles in the *Thirty Days with a Great Spiritual Teacher* series:

All Will Be Well
Based on the Classic Spirituality of *Julian of Norwich*

God Awaits You
Based on the Classic Spirituality of *Meister Eckhart*

Let Nothing Disturb You
A Journey to the Center of the Soul with *Teresa of Avila*

Peace of Heart
Based on the Life and Teachings of *Francis of Assisi*

True Serenity
Based on Thomas A Kempis' *The Imitation of Christ*

Simpy Surrender
Based on The Little Way of *Thérèse of Lisieux*

Where Only Love Can Go
A Journey of the Soul into *The Cloud of Unknowing*

You Shall Not Want
A Spiritual Journey Based on *The Psalms*

Living in the Presence of the Lord
Based on The Everyday Spirituality of *Brother Lawrence*

30 Days with a Great Spiritual Teacher

LET THERE BE LIGHT

Based on the Visionary Spirituality of
Hildegard of Bingen

AVE MARIA PRESS Notre Dame, Indiana 46556

John Kirvan is the editor and author of several books including *The Restless Believers*, and currently lives in southern California where he writes primarily about classical spirituality.

For this work, various writings of Hildegard of Bingen have been freely adapted into modern English. They have been combined, rearranged, and paraphrased to meet the needs of a meditational format.

Copyright © 1997 Quest Associates.
International Standard Book Number: 0-87793-602-1
Cover and text design by Elizabeth J. French.
Printed and bound in the United States of America.

Library of Congress Cataloging-in-Publication Data
Kirvan, John J.
    Let there be light : based on the visionary spirituality of Hildegard of Bingen / by John Kirvan.
          p.   cm. — (30 days with a great spiritual teacher)
    ISBN 0-87793-602-1
    1. Devotional calendars.   I. Hildegard, Saint, 1098-1179.   II. Title.   III. Series.
BV4811.K47   1997
  242'.2—dc21   96-49862
                                                        CIP

Contents

Let those who live
with eyes wide open
and hear with open ears
welcome with love
these mystical words
which have come from him
who is Life.

–Hildegard of Bingen

Hildegard of Bingen

Hildegard of Bingen (1098–1179) has penetrated today's consciousness, gaining not only media celebrity, but almost cult status. Among many who laud her are some who would otherwise never dream of associating with an aristocratic, visionary abbess of the twelfth century, or for that matter with anything even vaguely resembling religion. In many cases her biggest fans are either unaware of her religious status or prefer to ignore it in favor of the extraordinary talents and accomplishments that have made her a source of inspiration and admiration.

The fascination is understandable. She was a mystic (perhaps Germany's first) and a visionary, but she was also a prophet, a reformer, a scientist, an encyclopedist, a composer, and a dramatist—a Renaissance personality well before the Renaissance.

Her *Book of Simple Medicine* is an encyclopedia of natural science.

Add to it her four books on animals, two on herbs and trees, three on gems and metals, and you are still describing only a part of her productivity and a narrow segment of her wide-ranging interests. But it is a part that plays directly to today's interest in natural medicine and holistic health. Her accomplishments as a composer and dramatist focus special attention on her at a time when there is a worldwide effort to recover the neglected works of many all-but-invisible women composers.

Her time, without question, has come.

Sometimes lost in the flurry of admiration for her more measurable achievements is her powerful spiritual vision. As in so many other things, she is unique here as well. She differs greatly from those mystics who wrote out of an intense personal experience of God and whose lives are the stuff of their message. Rather than a mystic, Hildegard is more properly seen as a visionary and a prophet. The language she uses to describe her visions also differs from that of her contemporaries. Bernard of Clairvaux, for example, uses lush, romantic, even erotic language. Hildegard's writing, on the other hand, is controlled, rational, even cool in style. Nor does she employ the "divine-spouse" approach to spirituality, often associated with women mystics whose words have come to us through the courtesy of their male spiritual directors.

Hildegard's visions are wide-ranging. She views heaven and earth, their history and their future, in the coded language of images. She reports what she has seen and then decodes the imagery in commentaries that are often long and whose theology is extraordinarily complex. She ranges with equal authority, self-confidence, and painstaking detail from the fall of the angels to rules for the marriage bed.

There is no attempt in this book to summarize the breadth of her visions and prophecies. Rather the aim is to bring together passages of spiritual wisdom from many different places in her writings. Hopefully, her insight can be of special help to us as we seek to penetrate the mystery of God and to live consciously in his presence day by day.

More specifically, we have chosen the theme of contrast between night and day, light and darkness. You will find the theme explicitly in the short visionary passages which begin each day of meditative prayer and in the reading that spells out the vision. In a special way, you will find it in the exercises suggested for the end of the day. Each of these invites you to enter a dark place, and there to reach out in your imagination to touch the face of God.

The days begin with the images shown to Hildegard. They end asking you to trust your own imagination. This may be very hard.

Most of us have come to believe that imagination is synonymous with the fantasy life of a child, the kind of fantasy we are expected to outgrow. Rather than exploring the imagination as a passage to sturdy, serviceable truth, spiritual and otherwise, we are expected to outgrow it.

But imagination carries us beyond the captivity of what is easily seen to what could be, to what can be, to what most surely is beyond where our senses end and faith begins.

And it is precisely on this journey that Hildegard is such helpful guide.

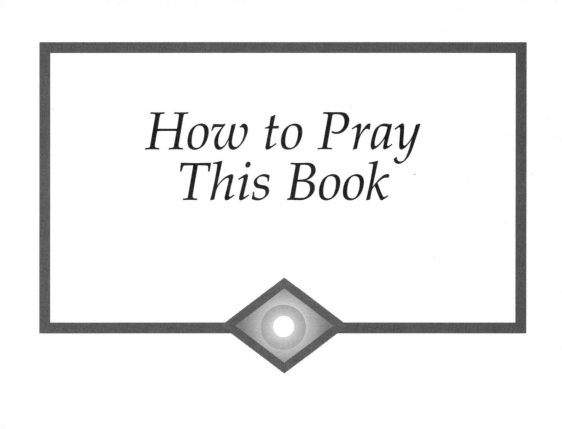

*How to Pray
This Book*

The purpose of this book is to open a gate for you, to make accessible the spiritual insight and wisdom of one of history's most important visionaries and prophets, Hildegard of Bingen.

This is not a book for mere reading. It invites you to meditate and pray its words on a daily basis over a period of thirty days, and in a special way to enter into prayer through the unique doorway of Hildegard's visionary experiences, and your own imagination.

It is a handbook for a special kind of spiritual journey.

Before you read the "rules" for taking this journey, remember that this book is meant to free your spirit, not confine it. If on any day the meditation does not resonate well for you, turn elsewhere to find a passage which seems to best fit the spirit of your day and your soul. Don't hesitate to repeat a day as often as you like until you feel that you have discovered what the Spirit, through the words of the author, has to say to your spirit.

Here are some suggestions on one way to use this book as a cornerstone of your prayers, based on the three forms of prayer central to Western spiritual tradition: the lesson, the meditation, and the petition. The author of the classic *Cloud of Unknowing* has written that "they might better be called reading, reflecting, and praying. These three are so linked together that there can be no profitable reflection without first reading or hearing. Nor will beginners or even the spiritually adept come to true prayer without first taking time to reflect on what they have heard or read."

So for these thirty days there are daily, two-part readings developed from the writings of Hildegard for the beginning of the day. Each begins, as was her style, with a fragment of one of her visionary experiences which is followed by a commentary. There is a meditation in the form of a mantra to carry with you for reflection throughout the day. And there is an exercise for bringing your day to an end. It requires you to find a place of quiet dark where you might enter into a meditation of the imagination and a final petitionary prayer.

But the forms and suggestions are not meant to become a straitjacket. Go where the Spirit leads you.

As Your Day Begins

As the day begins, set aside a quiet moment in a quiet place to do the reading provided for the day.

The passage is short. Its two parts, prophecy and commentary, never run more than a couple of hundred words. They have been carefully selected to give a spiritual focus, a spiritual center, to your whole day. They are designed to remind you, as another day begins, of your own existence at a spiritual level. They are meant to put you in the presence of the spiritual master who is your companion and teacher on this journey. But most of all, the purpose of the passage is to remind you that at this moment and at every moment during this day you will be living and acting in the presence of a God who invites you continually, but quietly, to live in and through him.

Do not attempt to understand fully the visionary passage that begins each reading. Don't be surprised if you understand nothing. Understanding is not the point. Try rather to implant in your imagination the images that it conjures up. They are not meant to be clear analogies or visual examples. They are what they are, a segment of a very mysterious experience from the life of Hildegard, a clouded entry into the mind of God. It will take time, perhaps a long time, for you to become comfortable with prophetic images as a route into prayer. In this program you will be invited to exercise your own imagination when you come to the close of each day. The effort may be exasperating, but it could also be an unusually rewarding spiritual experience. The second part of the reading is a more traditional passage that appeals more to the understanding than to the imagination.

A word of advice: proceed slowly. Very slowly. The passages have been broken down into sense lines to help you do just this. Don't read to get to the end, but to savor each word, each phrase, each image. There is no predicting, no determining in advance, what short phrase, what word, will trigger a response in your spirit. Give God a chance. After all you are not reading these passages, you are praying them. You are establishing a mood of spiritual attentiveness for your whole day. What's the rush?

All Through Your Day

Immediately following the day's reading you will find a single sentence, a meditation in the form of a mantra, a word borrowed from the Hindu tradition. This phrase is meant as a companion for your spirit as it moves through a busy day. Write it down on a 3"x 5" card or on the appropriate page of your daybook. Look at it as often as you can. Repeat it quietly to yourself and go on your way.

It is not meant to stop you in your tracks or to distract you from responsibilities, but simply, gently, to remind you of the presence of God and your desire to respond to this presence.

You might consider carrying with you the mantra from the day's reading in order to let its imagery sink more deeply into your imagination. Resist the urge to pull it apart and to make clean, clear rational sense of it. An image is not an idea. But it is a way of knowing God in a manner that emphasizes that the object of our search is immeasurably mysterious.

As Your Day Is Ending

This is a time for letting go of the day, for entering a world of imaginative prayer.

Choose a quiet, dark place that you can return to each day at its ending. When you come to it, your first task is to quiet your spirit. Sit, or if you are comfortable doing so, kneel. Do whatever stills your soul. Breathe deeply. Inhale, exhale—slowly and deliberately, again and again until you feel your body let go of its tension.

Now, using the least possible light, follow the evening exercise slowly, phrase by phrase, stopping as it suggests. If you find your mind arguing with it, analyzing it, trying to figure out its meanings and goals, don't be surprised. Simply start again by quieting your mind and freeing your imagination. Put behind you, as best you can, all that consciously or unconsciously stands between you and God.

This exercise is not meant to last more than a few minutes. End it when you are comfortable doing so. Then turn to the familiarity of a final prayer of the day, a petition based on the comforting, healing words of Psalm 36. In this way, a simple evening prayer gathers together the spiritual character of the day that is now ending as it began, in the presence of God.

It is a time for summary and closure. Invite God to embrace you with love and to protect you through the night.

Sleep well.

Some Other Ways to Use This Book

1. Use it any way your spirit suggests. As mentioned earlier, skip a passage that doesn't resonate for you on a given day, or repeat for a second day or even several days, a passage whose richness speaks to you. The truths of a spiritual life are not absorbed in a day, or for that matter, in a lifetime. So take your time. Be patient with the Lord. Be patient with yourself.

2. Take two passages and/or their mantras—the more contrasting the better—and "bang" them together. Spend time discovering how their similarities or differences illumine your path.

3. Start a spiritual journal to record and deepen your experience of this thirty-day journey. Using either the mantra or another phrase from the reading that appeals to you, write a spiritual

account of your day, a spiritual reflection. Create your own meditation.

4. Join millions who are seeking to deepen their spiritual life by joining with others to form a small group. More and more people are doing just this to support each other in their mutual quest. Meet once a week, or at least every other week, to discuss and pray about one of the meditations. There are many books and guides available to help you make such a group effective.

Thirty Days with
Hildegard of Bingen

Day One

———————◆◆◆◆———————

My Day Begins

*Even though I lack
the strength of lions and their courage,
and am but Adam's fragile rib
graced with a mystical spirit,
I saw
a blazing fire,
incomprehensible, inextinguishable,
totally alive, Life itself.*

I heard a voice from on high:
"Even though you are
among the least of my creatures,
and as a woman, unlettered,
ill prepared to read literature
with scholarly understanding,
I have nonetheless touched you with my light,
which kindles in you
a fire hot as the burning sun;
Speak out and tell the world all that I show you.
Do not be timid.
Speak out about those things
that through my Spirit
I have spoken to you,
and you have come to understand.

Do not be like those
who should have shown my people the true way,
but who perversely have remained silent
about the justice they have come to know,
unwilling to deny the evil desires
that cling to them like masters
and make them avoid the face of the Lord,
ashamed to speak the truth.
You, whom I have taught
by mystical inspiration,
even though you are trodden down
by the masculine sex,
speak openly and always of that
fire you have seen
and that burns within you.

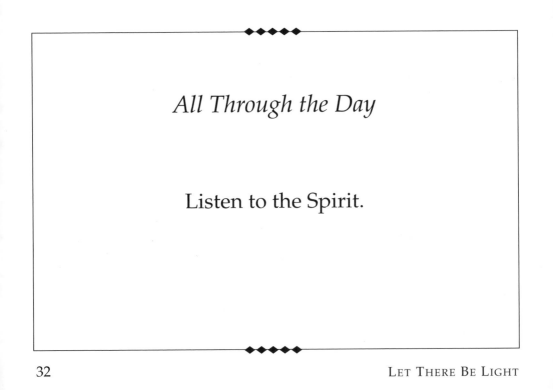

All Through the Day

Listen to the Spirit.

My Day Is Ending

Spend a moment welcoming the dark.
Make friends with the silence of the night.

Silence has its own voice.
Darkness has its own face.
Quiet the voices of the day that are still with you.
Listen for the Spirit.

Be quiet. Listen.
Let the dark show you its face.
You will know when it is time for words.
Speak softly. Speak slowly.
You will be heard.

Night Prayer

How precious to me is your steadfast love, O God!
I take refuge in the shadow of your wings
and feast on the abundance of your table.
I depend on the river of your gifts.
For with you is the fountain of life;
only in your light do I see light.
Amen.

Day Two

◆◆◆◆◆

My Day Begins

I saw
a single block of iron-colored stone,
broader and higher than I could measure,
with a white cloud above it;
and above the cloud a royal throne,
round in shape, on which the One who is, was sitting,
shining brightly and majestically in his glory,
and so bright
that I could not see him without difficulty.

The stone that I saw
represents the enormous fear of God
which should forever permeate the hearts
of even the greatest saints.

I saw it as a single block of stone,
enormously broad and high and the color of iron.
We cannot ignore it or shove it aside.
It has immense breadth
because God is incomprehensible,
and height because his divinity
transcends everything else,
exceeding the farthest range of our senses.

I saw that the white cloud above that stone
represented human wisdom,
and the royal throne above the cloud,

the strong faith of the Christian people.
For wherever the fear of the Lord takes root,
human wisdom will also appear
and faith will emerge.
For when God is feared,
he is understood by faith aided by human wisdom.
In them, together, God takes his place,
supreme above all else.
Neither the power of our minds nor the force of our wills
can comprehend him
but only single-minded and open faith
in One who is
above everything, everyone else.

All Through the Day

Faith begins in awe.

My Day Is Ending

Spend a moment welcoming the dark.
Make friends with the silence of the night.

In the space around you,
reconstruct the stone that Hildegard saw.
Begin small. Then let it grow.
Let it widen until it reaches from wall to wall.
Let it grow from floor to ceiling.
Imagine a larger room, a wider room, a higher room.
Watch the stone fill whatever space you can imagine.
It is beyond your power to contain
or to measure.

Night Prayer

How precious to me is your steadfast love, O God!
I take refuge in the shadow of your wings
and feast on the abundance of your table.
I depend on the river of your gifts.
For with you is the fountain of life;
only in your light do I see light.
Amen.

Day Three

◆◆◆◆◆

My Day Begins

*I saw
the One who is seated upon his throne,
the Center of a great circle of light
as golden as a dawn,
as wide
and as incomprehensible.*

This means
that from the Father,
whose strength encircles all things,
there goes out a stream of his creation.

We are meant to see
that he does all things through his Son,
who is always with him
in the majesty of his Godhead,
ordaining and perfecting all things
through him
who preceded all worlds,
and who was in the world from the beginning.

His Son glows
with the brilliant beauty of the dawn;
for by the power of the Holy Spirit

he took flesh from that wisest of virgins,
who is the dawn.

We will never comprehend
the full extent of his glory,
for no creature can or should have
a standard of goodness or power
with which to measure the power of God or his deeds.

Let us approach the living God,
who reigns over all things,
who shines
in the goodness and wonder of his creation.

All Through the Day

How shall we measure the Dawn?

My Day Is Ending

Spend a moment welcoming the dark.
Make friends with the silence of the night.

Let the night fill every corner of the room
until it is complete.
Now light a single candle
in the farthest, deepest corner of the silent darkness.
Return to your place. Close your eyes.
Let the darkness deepen.

Open your eyes.
Let the light grow
until everything in the room
absorbs the glow of this one small flame.
It is the Dawn.
How shall we measure it?

Night Prayer

How precious to me is your steadfast love, O God!
I take refuge in the shadow of your wings
and feast on the abundance of your table.
I depend on the river of your gifts.
For with you is the fountain of life;
only in your light do I see light.
Amen.

Day Four

My Day Begins

I saw
the One who is sitting on the throne,
holding to his breast
what looked like
a lump of black and filthy clay
as big as a human heart,
decorated with precious stones and pearls.

In the lump of dark, muddy clay
we are meant to see ourselves—
widely different from each other,
full of defects,
stupid and blind,
impervious to the good things of the Lord,
blithely ignoring what we should praise,
preferring what we should abhor.

When we should be doing the works of justice,
we choose, often as not, the works of evil.

But God our Father,
contemplating this lump of clay
like any father,
hugs us, his children,
close to his breast.

Because he is God
he has the tender love
of a father for his children.
Indeed, so great is his love for us
that he sent his only Son to the cross,
like a meek lamb carried to the slaughter.
And his Son brought back
the lost sheep,
bearing them on his shoulders,
precious stones and pearls
with which to grace
the lump of dark clay
that he hugs to his breast.

All Through the Day

We are clay,
and unto clay we shall return.

My Day Is Ending

Spend a moment welcoming the dark and the silence.
Make friends with the silence of the night.

Bring with you into the night a handful of your day
. . . a ball of crumpled papers
that have passed through your hands,
a child's toy, an empty plate,
whatever is the ordinary stuff of your life.
Discover, caress, its uneven shape,
its creases and crevices, the record of its passage.
Hold it to your breast.
Embrace it. Embrace yourself.
Feel the embrace of God.

Night Prayer

How precious to me is your steadfast love, O God!
I take refuge in the shadow of your wings
and feast on the abundance of your table.
I depend on the river of your gifts.
For with you is the fountain of life;
only in your light do I see light.
Amen.

Day Five

◆◆◆◆◆

My Day Begins

I saw
a figure so bright and glorious
that I could not look at her face or her garments.
She looked upon the pilgrims
who came from the world and entered the building
where they put on their new garments,
and she said to each of them:
"Think about the garment you have put on,
and do not forget the Creator who made you."

❧

In the blindingly beautiful woman,
Virtue stands before us,
beckoning to us,
terrible as lightning,
welcome as the sun.

Her awesome beauty and her gentleness
are incomprehensible.
The god-like brilliance of her face,
the shining beauty of her garments
are blinding.
But she is within us and within everyone,
sustaining us,
turning away from no one,
even when we resist her every advance.

Those who follow her
are those who have chosen
to leave behind their unbelief
and their sinful choices,
to put on a new garment of eternal life.
To them, to us, she says:
"Do not turn back."

But if we should falter and stray,
we can still return to God our Creator.
Let those who have ears, hear!

All Through the Day

Do not turn back.

My Day Is Ending

Spend a moment welcoming the dark and the silence.
Make friends with the silence of the night.

Welcome her who stands
just out of reach—
beckoning, worrying, welcoming, demanding.

Name her.

Is she Truth? Charity? Faith? Hope?
Sobriety? Fidelity? Honesty?

Name her . . . approach her.

Embrace her.

Night Prayer

How precious to me is your steadfast love, O God!
I take refuge in the shadow of your wings
and feast on the abundance of your table.
I depend on the river of your gifts.
For with you is the fountain of life;
only in your light do I see light.
Amen.

Day Six

My Day Begins

I saw
a head, the color of flames,
licking, flame-like,
at a terrifying, anger-filled face.

It was silent.
It was still.
It was terrible to see.

It was the face of a jealous God.
We are born, each of us,
with a desire for good
and a lust for evil.
We are called to life
and attracted to death.
We hear: "Do good."
And we respond: "Choose pleasure."

We embrace bitterness,
stealing from ourselves a treasury of good
and laying up a treasury of evil.

A jealous God sees us
and turns a terrible face to us.
But rather than condemning us,
he calls us to penitence,

he recalls us to life.
He uses his power sparingly,
with mercy,
never slaying, but breathing new life,
hearing our prayers.

I know what I deserve.
Your mercy humbles me,
but gives glory to your name.

All Through the Day

Your mercy humbles me.

LET THERE BE LIGHT

My Day Is Ending

Spend a moment welcoming the dark.
Make friends with the silence of the night.

Make friends with its faces.
Do not cower in the corner of the night,
but recall the saddened face of someone you have hurt.
Ask for forgiveness.
Recall the face of someone who has loved you,
who may still love you.
Ask for the love to last;
ask for forgiveness.
Search out the jealous face of God.
Ask for mercy.
Hear it given.
Accept it.

Night Prayer

How precious to me is your steadfast love, O God!
I take refuge in the shadow of your wings
and feast on the abundance of your table.
I depend on the river of your gifts.
For with you is the fountain of life;
only in your light do I see light.
Amen.

Day Seven

My Day Begins

*I saw
a radiantly beautiful figure,
full of eyes on every side,
totally alive,
changing its form like a cloud,
becoming now wider,
now narrower.*

Sometimes, when God reaches out to us,
we disdain him
and put off repenting until our body is reduced to old age,
and we get tired of sinning.
Then God admonishes and urges us again
to do good and resist evil.
Even if we ignore his new approach,
we often have goodness forced, so to speak, upon us.
Money and other problems overtake us.
We can't do what we planned to do
when we were prosperous.
Even so, God does not forsake us.
After all,
he did not labor wholly in vain within us.
His gracious pity shows itself in our lives
in an abundance of mercy and compassion,

looking upon the sorrows
of all who attempt to follow him.
He is with us to console and save our souls,
to prepare us for eternal life,
not eternal death.
His grace goes before us
so that the good may not fall,
and sinners may rise again.
His grace precedes and follows us,
touches and warms us,
so that we can, with passion,
receive and fulfill his words of life.

All Through the Day

God does not labor in vain.

My Day Is Ending

Spend a moment welcoming the dark.
Make friends with the silence of the night.

Fill the night room with friendly faces;
decorate it with fantasies.
Look around.
Reach out to touch what you have.
Listen hard.
Can you hear the future above the noise?

Night Prayer

How precious to me is your steadfast love, O God!
I take refuge in the shadow of your wings
and feast on the abundance of your table.
I depend on the river of your gifts.
For with you is the fountain of life;
only in your light do I see light.
Amen.

Day Eight

My Day Begins

I heard him say:
"Let my sheep be attentive
to the words of their shepherd.
Let those who live
with eyes wide open
and hear with open ears
welcome with love
these mystical words
which have come from him
who is Life."

If someone who loved you very much
gave you a great treasure,
and said to you:
"Profit from this, grow rich,
but let everyone know who gave you this treasure,"
you would work very hard at
fulfilling his request.

This is what your Creator has done.
He loves you greatly
for you are his creature
and he has given you great treasures.
But with his gifts
comes the condition
that you apply his gifts to good works,
that you grow in virtue.

Your task then
is to make your gift valuable to others
through works of justice,
so that your life and deeds
will mirror their Giver.

Choose what is good,
do even greater deeds,
and glorify your Father
who has lavished you
with his gifts.

All Through the Day

Be generous with his gifts.

My Day Is Ending

Spend a moment welcoming the dark.
Make friends with the silence of the night.

Fill the room with the gifts that have flooded your life—
your home, your health, your intelligence, your family.
Picture the room boarded up, airless.
Watch the gifts dry up, stagnate,
wilt even as they are protected from the world.

Now break down the walls,
let in the light and air,
let in the world.
Let in God.
Welcome his creatures.
Distribute his gifts.

Night Prayer

How precious to me is your steadfast love, O God!
I take refuge in the shadow of your wings
and feast on the abundance of your table.
I depend on the river of your gifts.
For with you is the fountain of life;
only in your light do I see light.
Amen.

Day Nine

My Day Begins

I saw
pavement surrounding the building
that was like white glass
shining with calm splendor.
But the splendor of the One
who is seated on the throne
showing me all these things
shone even more brightly,
piercing the pavement
even into the abyss.

This is to say
that it is the strength of
crystal pure, clear, open faith
and mirror-like simplicity
that undergirds and expands
the task of building the city of God,
and all the life and creations within it.
So when we begin to do good works
with the calm and luminous intention of faith,
we touch God;
and when our works are perfected in faith,
we come to know him profoundly.

For when God's work is accomplished in us,
faith is the mark of the perfection
with which each of us has sought God.

LET THERE BE LIGHT

For the grace of almighty God
who rules all and manifests to us all things
through the fortitude of our faith
reduces the devil
to nothingness and death.
God's power
pierces the darkness of unbelief
with the pure faith
that is born again of the Spirit and water.

All Through the Day

Help my unbelief.

My Day Is Ending

Spend a moment welcoming the dark.
Make friends with the silence of the night.

With your imagination summon up the skyline
of a great city.
Now close in on a busy street
in the first hours of a working day.
You are on that street.
God is here too,
at work.
Feel his presence throughout the city—
throughout this room.
Greet him.
Reach out and touch him.

Night Prayer

How precious to me is your steadfast love, O God!
I take refuge in the shadow of your wings
and feast on the abundance of your table.
I depend on the river of your gifts.
For with you is the fountain of life;
only in your light do I see light.
Amen.

Day Ten

My Day Begins

*I saw
at the time of creation
a vast array of bright, vital lamps
of fiery brilliance
and unclouded splendor.*

Those who are deeply committed to God
and burn with true love and affection
for their Creator
enjoy heavenly beatitude.
But those who fake the service of God
not only fail to advance to greater things,
but are justly deprived of everything
they presume to possess
on their own account
and are cast out of his presence.

The bright lights
are the vast army of heavenly spirits,
enjoying the blessed life and radiating great beauty
because they did not see
in their creation by God

a reason for pride,
but persisted in divine love.

They took on
a fiery brilliance,
an unclouded splendor,
because unlike Lucifer and his followers
who chose to rebel against their Creator,
they clothed themselves
with the vibrant colors of divine love
instead of the dull, lackluster shades of rejection.

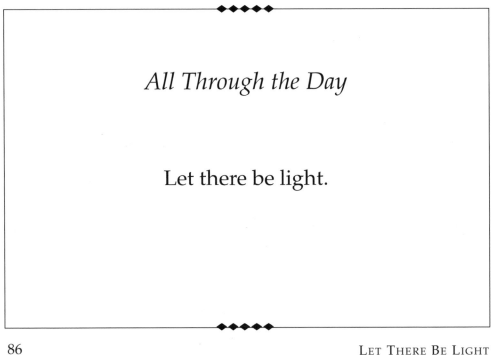

All Through the Day

Let there be light.

My Day Is Ending

Spend a moment welcoming the dark.
Make friends with the silence of the night.

Let the darkness of the room
become the darkness at the beginning of creation.
There, in a corner, is a first trace of light.
It expands, spreading wide and high. Slowly.

And in it we begin to see ourselves,
emerging from the darkness.
We are not the light,
our light is reflected light.
Now welcome the light
in which we sit, and stand and walk and grow.
Welcome God's light.

Night Prayer

How precious to me is your steadfast love, O God!
I take refuge in the shadow of your wings
and feast on the abundance of your table.
I depend on the river of your gifts.
For with you is the fountain of life;
only in your light do I see light.
Amen.

Day Eleven

My Day Begins

I saw
a woman bowed to the ground
under the assault
of many whirlwinds.
And I saw her regain her strength
pulling herself up,
resisting the winds
with great courage.

I will remember
that I am God's creation,
and I will not yield to the devil's promptings.
nor to the frailty of my humanity.

I will wage war.

When anger threatens to consume me,
I will look to the goodness of God
who is untouched by anger.
I will breathe the sweetness of his air,
enjoy the gentleness
with which he irrigates the earth.

When hatred threatens
to overcome me with darkness,
I will look to God's mercy and remember

the martyrdom
of his Son.
I will reassure myself
by recalling
that roses grow with thorns.

And I will acknowledge
that I have been redeemed.

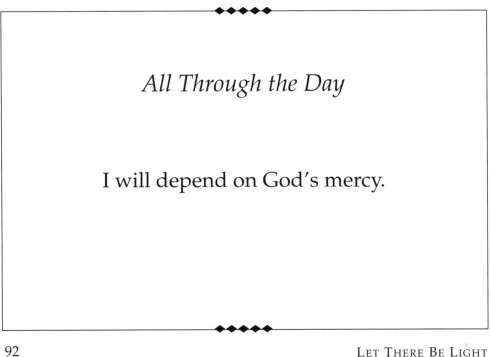

All Through the Day

I will depend on God's mercy.

My Day Is Ending

Spend a moment welcoming the dark.
Make friends with the silence of the night.

See yourself in a single figure
that emerges in the darkness.
Look at your face.
Imagine anger so twisting your features
that it is nearly impossible to recognize yourself.
Or is it?

Imagine lines of hatred so deep
that they seem forever carved there.
Now surrender to your need for God's mercy.
Let God reshape the features of your life.
Feel the joy.

Night Prayer

How precious to me is your steadfast love, O God!
I take refuge in the shadow of your wings
and feast on the abundance of your table.
I depend on the river of your gifts.
For with you is the fountain of life;
only in your light do I see light.
Amen.

Day Twelve

My Day Begins

*I saw
a splendor,
dawn-like in its beauty,
containing within it
flashes of purple lightning.*

❧

When pride swells up within you,
and you want to position yourself
higher than the stars
and beyond all of God's faithful creatures,
you can be certain you will fall.
Pay attention:
do not forget the love
with which God has freed you,
or disregard the great gifts
that constantly flow from him.
Above all, do not forget
that as often as you have fallen into sin
and preferred death to life,
just as often he has called you back from death.

And if indeed you do forget all these things,

and out of pride fall again,
recall the words of scripture
and the wisdom of the fathers.
Pay attention as they tell you
to do good and avoid evil.

Confess:
"I have sinned greatly,
and I desire to return to you, my Father
who has created me."

He will receive you with an undiminished love,
take you to his bosom,
and hold you tightly to himself.

All Through the Day

You are forgiven.

My Day Is Ending

Spend a moment welcoming the dark.
Make friends with the silence of the night.

You are in an open field as this night begins.
There is a stone table.
Place on it all the moments of this day
in which you have allowed pride to overtake your soul.
In silence wait for the dawn.
It comes in splendor, rolling back the night,
filling the room with brilliance,
with flashes of purple lightning.
The table is bare.

Night Prayer

How precious to me is your steadfast love, O God!
I take refuge in the shadow of your wings
and feast on the abundance of your table.
I depend on the river of your gifts.
For with you is the fountain of life;
only in your light do I see light.
Amen.

Day Thirteen

My Day Begins

I saw
into secret places
at heaven's pinnacle
two armies of spirits,
both shining with great brightness.

Our almighty Father,
who has created all that is,
has in gracious wisdom willed
that each have its own proper place.

Some creatures he has destined to stay on earth.
Others are to inhabit the celestial regions.
He has also set in place the blessed angels,
both for human salvation
and the honor of his name.

This is why we see
in the secret places of heaven
two armies of spirits
shining with great brightness.
What our bodily eye cannot penetrate
we can see with our inner eye.

These two armies
represent the human body and soul
which together are destined
to enjoy eternal blessedness
with the citizens of heaven.
We are destined
to sing a glad and joyous song,
to live forever
with all those who have rejected injustice
and have done the works of justice.
We might have, at the suggestion of the devil,
done evil,
but we chose goodness instead.

All Through the Day

Choose justice.

LET THERE BE LIGHT

My Day Is Ending

Spend a moment welcoming the dark.
Make friends with the silence of the night.

Now let the silence be broken
by the voices,
that may have gone unheard
in the noisy corridors of your day—
the voices of those who seek justice.
Let them cut through the silence.
Give them a hearing.
Choose justice.

Night Prayer

How precious to me is your steadfast love, O God!
I take refuge in the shadow of your wings
and feast on the abundance of your table.
I depend on the river of your gifts.
For with you is the fountain of life;
only in your light do I see light.
Amen.

Day Fourteen

My Day Begins

I saw
a man as he caught the scent
of a beautiful white flower,
but he refused to taste it
or even to take it in his hands.
Instead he turned away
and fell into an undergrowth of darkness.

"Who does not know," as Job says,
"that everything that is,
has been made by the hand of the Lord,
that he holds in his hand
the soul of every living thing,
supplying the very breath of all who live?"

Who is there so dull
as not to be aware of how
the earth nourishes the plants
that provide fruit,
of how the fruit in turn
nourishes the animals,
of how the sky holds light and air,
of how the air holds the birds?

All of them testify
that they have been placed here
and are held here
by the strong hand
of a Universal Ruler
who in his strength
so provides for them
that they lack nothing
that they need.

So why then
is it so easy for us to forget
that we are part of that same creation,
dependent on that same strength,
provided for by that same generosity?

All Through the Day

The earth is the Lord's,
and all that is in it.

My Day Is Ending

Spend a moment welcoming the dark.
Make friends with the silence of the night.

Imagine a garden springing up in the darkness.
Let there be sun and light and birds.
Let the earth give birth to flowers and fruits.
Place yourself in the garden.
Breathe the air.
Eat the fruits.
Smell the flowers.
Give thanks to its Creator.
Acknowledge your dependence.

Night Prayer

How precious to me is your steadfast love, O God!
I take refuge in the shadow of your wings
and feast on the abundance of your table.
I depend on the river of your gifts.
For with you is the fountain of life;
only in your light do I see light.
Amen.

Day Fifteen

My Day Begins

I saw
people carrying earthen vessels
filled with milk
for making cheese.
Some of the milk was thick
and strong cheese was made from it,
but some was thin
and its cheese was weak.

❧

Strength is born of strength.

When, out of pride, I am tempted to build towers
without a firm foundation in rock
and persist in seeing myself
as shoulders above anyone else—
who will help me?

Where shall I turn
when the ancient serpent
who fell to his death by wishing
to be above everyone else
tries to bring me down with him into the depths?

Then I will find myself saying:
Where is my King?
Where is my God?

What good can I do without him?
None.

But then, if I look to God
who gave me life,
he will give me his strength
and nothing will be able
to conquer me.

I will come to know
with humility
the depths of his gift,
and I will rejoice
in his strength.

All Through the Day

I will rejoice in his strength.

My Day Is Ending

Spend a moment welcoming the dark.
Make friends with the silence of the night.

You are a child again on a beach.
You build a tower a handful of sand at a time.
Someone says: "Be careful. . . . "
Someone else says: "Why don't you . . . ?"
But this is going to be your tower, yours alone.
Watch it rise.
Watch it fall to the strength of the sea.
Where shall you turn?
How shall you begin again?
With what shall you begin?
On what will you rely?

Night Prayer

How precious to me is your steadfast love, O God!
I take refuge in the shadow of your wings
and feast on the abundance of your table.
I depend on the river of your gifts.
For with you is the fountain of life;
only in your light do I see light.
Amen.

Day Sixteen

―◆◆◆◆―

My Day Begins

I saw
a splendidly serene
four-cornered object
that pointed
to the four corners
of the earth.
It was
ablaze with many eyes.

I am a pilgrim.

Where am I?
"You are in the shadow of death."

On what path am I journeying?
"You are on the path of error."

What consolation do I have?
"You have only what a pilgrim has."

But I should have been
a companion to the angels,
for I am alive,
breathed into life by God
out of mud.
"But when you discovered
that you could turn your eyes in any direction,

you surrendered your sight and your joy,
and relinquished your inheritance
to choose slavery."
Where is my honor now?
Where am I?
How did I get here?

Who will comfort me in my captivity?
Who will have mercy on my afflictions?

Heaven hear my cry;
earth, tremble with my sorrow.

All Through the Day

Heaven, hear my cry.

LET THERE BE LIGHT

My Day Is Ending

Spend a moment welcoming the dark.
Make friends with the silence of the night.

Unroll across the floor of your imagination
a map tangled with streets and intersections.

First at one crossing, then at another,
and then at still more, there is a sign:
"You are here!"
But where is here?
How often have you been here?
How do you decide which way to turn?
Let heaven hear your cry.
Feel the earth tremble in sympathy.

Night Prayer

How precious to me is your steadfast love, O God!
I take refuge in the shadow of your wings
and feast on the abundance of your table.
I depend on the river of your gifts.
For with you is the fountain of life;
only in your light do I see light.
Amen.

Day Seventeen

My Day Begins

I saw
Humility
wearing on her breast a shining mirror
which reflected
with wondrous brightness
the image of God's incarnate Son.

I, Humility,
am the strength of truthful minds
and the slayer of proud hearts.
I began my ascent of the steep slope to heaven
at its lowest point,
unlike Lucifer who raised himself above himself
and fell beneath himself.
If you wish to imitate me,
to become my child
and embrace me as your mother,
to carry out my work,
you must start at the foundation.
Only gradually can you mount upward
from virtue to virtue,
with a gentle and serene attitude.
If you attempt to ascend

by taking hold
of the highest branch of the tree first,
more often than not
you will just as swiftly fall.

But if you
begin your climb
at the foot of the path
and proceed one step at a time,
you will not fall so easily,
so quickly.

All Through the Day

Every path begins at its foot.

My Day Is Ending

Spend a moment welcoming the dark.
Make friends with the silence of the night.

Summon up an image of a path
that begins at the foot
but which stretches into the darkness,
far beyond where your eye can take you.

Consider how tempting it would be
to save a thousand steps and find yourself at its end . . .
at this moment . . . effortlessly.

What do you expect at the end of your journey?
God? He is here.
As much in the journey's first cautious step
as in its last.

Night Prayer

How precious to me is your steadfast love, O God!
I take refuge in the shadow of your wings
and feast on the abundance of your table.
I depend on the river of your gifts.
For with you is the fountain of life;
only in your light do I see light.
Amen.

Day Eighteen

My Day Begins

I saw
all the elements of the world
which until now
had existed in great calm
become suddenly agitated
and shaken with fear.

You have been made
in the image and likeness of God.
So don't be foolish.
How could this great honor
that has been given to you
escape being tested
as though it were valueless?
Gold must be tested in fire.
Precious stones,
in order to be smooth,
are first polished.
Everything of value
must be put to the test.
Of all creatures,
we are to be tested the most thoroughly.

Our spirit will be tested by spirit.
Our flesh by flesh,
good by evil,
sweetness by bitterness,
light by darkness,
life by death.
Before we are received in heaven,
we must expect
to be tested
by every creature
in heaven, on earth, and in hell.

So do not think your testing is unjust.
The reason for much is hidden from our eyes.
We are not wiser than God.

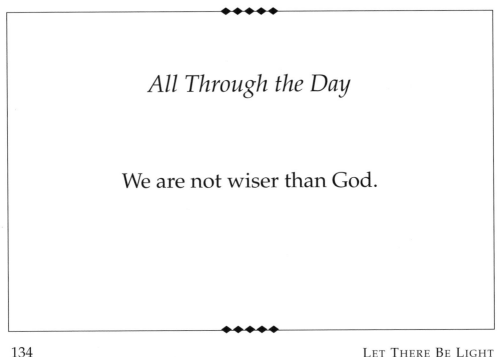

All Through the Day

We are not wiser than God.

My Day Is Ending

Spend a moment welcoming the dark.
Make friends with the silence of the night.

If not today, then yesterday or the day before.
Perhaps just an hour ago:
your soul has been tested.
Here in the dark recreate that moment.
Don't judge it.
Just seek to understand and accept it.
What about you was tested?
What happened that changed
just another moment into a test?
Were you caught by surprise?
Are you different now?

Night Prayer

How precious to me is your steadfast love, O God!
I take refuge in the shadow of your wings
and feast on the abundance of your table.
I depend on the river of your gifts.
For with you is the fountain of life;
only in your light do I see light.
Amen.

Day Nineteen

My Day Begins

I saw
surrounded by great brightness
a white cloud
that contained within itself
a multitude of stars.

❦

For the glory of God
and your salvation,
pursue humility and charity.
Armed with them,
you will never need to fear
the devil's snares,
but shall enjoy eternal life.

Humility is the soul,
and charity is the body
of your life with God.

They can no more be separated from each other
than your soul from your body
if you are to remain alive.
And just as the various parts of the body
and its many functions

are inseparably joined to the soul and the body,
so also all the other virtues
are dependent for their existence
on humility and charity.

Arm yourself, therefore, with the humility
of the child born in a manger
to a poor maiden.
And the charity
of that same Son of God,
who spurned no one,
neither publican, nor sinner,
but who sought in his humble love
to save all.

All Through the Day

God-like love is a humble love.

My Day Is Ending

Spend a moment welcoming the dark.
Make friends with the silence of the night.

Here in the dark, think of some things
that belong together and which, without each other,
are not only lifeless, but contradictory.

Think of proud love, of loveless humility.

And think of any combination of virtues:
of courage, of prudence,
even of hope.
But without humility, without love.

Now watch the life drain out.

Night Prayer

How precious to me is your steadfast love, O God!
I take refuge in the shadow of your wings
and feast on the abundance of your table.
I depend on the river of your gifts.
For with you is the fountain of life;
only in your light do I see light.
Amen.

Day Twenty

My Day Begins

I saw snow,
splendid in its whiteness,
but beneath its splendor
I saw
a murky darkness.

"I know your works,"
records John:
" . . . you are neither cold nor hot."
We have not, it is true,
surrendered to works of bloodless evil,
but on the other hand
we are not in fiery pursuit of goodness.
We are like those who stare into an abyss
so deep that we cannot find its bottom,
but who also raise our eyes
to mountain tops that are unreachable.
And we stand between them,
wavering, unsettled, and uncommitted.

We are like mild, soft winds
that blow, but bring no nourishment

to any living thing.

We begin, but we do not finish.

We touch the surface of good,
but never feed on its perfection.
We breathe the appetizing aroma of food,
but never let it reach our lips
or fill our belly.

We are in danger of withering from apathy,
of becoming an empty reed.

All Through the Day

He knows our works.

My Day Is Ending

Spend a moment welcoming the dark.
Make friends with the silence of the night.

At your feet
the floor falls away and a yawning crevice opens
to which there seems no bottom.
Attraction mingles with dread.

On its far side a mountain rises
far beyond the ceiling of the room,
far beyond where even your imagination can take you.
Attraction mingles with dread.

What now?
Paralysis? Half life?
Or a single, first, bold step?

Night Prayer

How precious to me is your steadfast love, O God!
I take refuge in the shadow of your wings
and feast on the abundance of your table.
I depend on the river of your gifts.
For with you is the fountain of life;
only in your light do I see light.
Amen.

Day Twenty-One

My Day Begins

*I saw
a great wheel
spinning from the east to the north,
and to the west and to the south,
and back towards the east
to the One who is on the throne.*

The power of God
extends to the four corners of the earth
encircling every creature in his embrace.
For all things
have been conceived by the Father
in union with the Son
and through the Holy Spirit.

We feel him in our bones, in the center of our souls.

We glimpse his presence
at the four corners of the earth:
in the east where justice begins,
in the north
where evil is thrown into confusion,
in the west
where darkness tries daily to overturn light,

only to have it rise again.
And in the south
where justice inflames the hearts of believers.

In time his work will be finished,
the last encircling of his creation completed.
Time will have been perfected.
The final day shall have arrived.
And we shall see at last
the perfect power and works
of him who was, and is and ever shall be,
who is without beginning and without end.

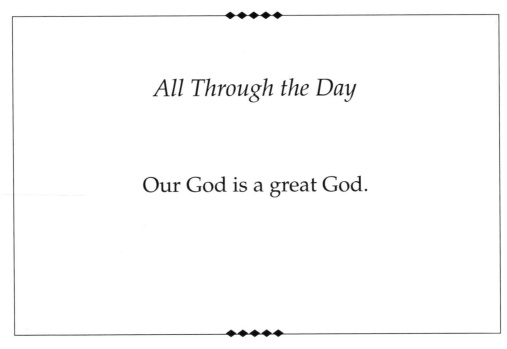

All Through the Day

Our God is a great God.

LET THERE BE LIGHT

My Day Is Ending

Spend a moment welcoming the dark.
Make friends with the silence of the night.

Bring an empty box with you into the darkness,
or create one from your imagination.
Open it. Place God in it.
Will he fit?
The box is too small, is it not?
Imagine a larger box . . .
the size of the room in which you are ending your day.
Still too small?
But the temptation is great
to shrink God to our size.

Now break the box down; break through the walls.
Let God be God-size.

Night Prayer

How precious to me is your steadfast love, O God!
I take refuge in the shadow of your wings
and feast on the abundance of your table.
I depend on the river of your gifts.
For with you is the fountain of life;
only in your light do I see light.
Amen.

Day Twenty-Two

My Day Begins

I saw
a globe struggling
to be free
of its bonds,
and with a groan
throwing them off.

Faced with the road to heaven
or the slippery slope into sin,
you know which you should choose.

But if you make the wrong choice
and fall into sin,
rise quickly,
confess your failure, and do penance.

If you are wounded,
don't you seek a physician
rather than die?

Likewise if you sin,
why would you not seek out your Father
who can deliver you from death?
When evil stirs in you

let your Father's love
reach into the very heart of your being
and ask him to help you,
by taking away the evil from your path
and giving you the strength to do good.
If an enemy were to capture you,
you would turn quickly
to anyone who could help you.
Do the same thing
when evil overtakes you.
Turn to your Father.
Beg, pray,
resolve to change,
and he will help you.

All Through the Day

God will help you.

LET THERE BE LIGHT

My Day Is Ending

Spend a moment welcoming the dark.
Make friends with the silence of the night.
Here in the gathering silence
make a list of the things that hold you captive . . .
a memory, a habit, a person, a place.
Choose one.
What needs to be done to break its hold?
Where do you need to turn for help?
What holds you back?

Night Prayer

How precious to me is your steadfast love, O God!
I take refuge in the shadow of your wings
and feast on the abundance of your table.
I depend on the river of your gifts.
For with you is the fountain of life;
only in your light do I see light.
Amen.

Day Twenty-Three

◆◆◆◆◆

My Day Begins

*I saw
a radiant light
as bright as the dawn
with a deep purple glow
shining through
which was the mystery
of God's incarnate Son.*

❧

No one hides a fountain.
They put it in plain view
so that everyone who is thirsty
can find it easily.
So too the Son of God is not hidden
or the path to him obstructed.
He is in plain sight,
ready to listen to your every request.

Therefore, in faith,
walk up to God, ask his mercy
and it will be given to you.

But if you do not seek him,
you will not find him.

A fountain is of no use

to someone who knows of it,
but who doesn't come to drink its waters.

You must approach if you wish to drink.
If you approach God
through the law
he has established for you,
you will find him.
The bread of life
and the water of salvation
will be given to you.

You will no longer hunger or thirst.

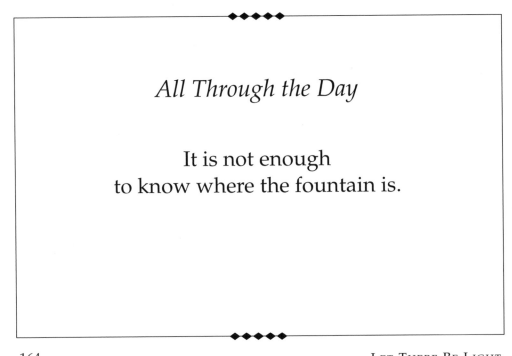

All Through the Day

It is not enough
to know where the fountain is.

LET THERE BE LIGHT

My Day Is Ending

Spend a moment welcoming the dark.
Make friends with the silence of the night.

The path to God's Son,
the Living Water, our Bread of Life,
was never meant to be obstructed.
Look across the room to a fountain
and to the figure who stands there beckoning you.
Imagine the path that stretches between you.

Is it obstructed?
With what?

Who blocked the path?

Who will clear it?

Night Prayer

How precious to me is your steadfast love, O God!
I take refuge in the shadow of your wings
and feast on the abundance of your table.
I depend on the river of your gifts.
For with you is the fountain of life;
only in your light do I see light.
Amen.

Day Twenty-Four

My Day Begins

I saw
three figures
standing together
and on the breast of the middle figure
there were two windows,
and above them an antlered deer.

The middle figure was Constancy—
perseverance in good works—
the pillar and the rampart
of the virtues,
the foundation of our inner life,
the discipline that leads us to God.

To be constant,
to persevere in good works,
means that we do not change directions
with every passing whim of the heart,
nor shake like the leaves of a tree
with every wind gust.

To be constant,
to persevere in good works,
is to abide in the true Rock,

which is the Son of God.

And as long as you persevere
in an immovable God,
who can move you?
Who can harm you?
The strong? The weak?
Princes or nobles? The rich or the poor?
No one. No thing.
Not so long as you build your life
on a true and solid foundation,
and avoid those whose sandy foundation
subjects them to every wind of temptation
and who never come to rest
on solid ground.

All Through the Day

Who can move me?

My Day Is Ending

Spend a moment welcoming the dark.
Make friends with the silence of the night.

In the very middle of the darkness
construct a pillar that goes from floor to ceiling,
as round, as strong, as your imagination can make it.

Recall images of storms, of earthquakes, of tornadoes.
Watch the pillar as it is lashed and battered.

Watch it remain where you built it.
Whatever happens around it,
it is constant.

Night Prayer

How precious to me is your steadfast love, O God!
I take refuge in the shadow of your wings
and feast on the abundance of your table.
I depend on the river of your gifts.
For with you is the fountain of life;
only in your light do I see light.
Amen.

Day Twenty-Five

My Day Begins

I saw
a pillar
enclosing a ladder,
and all the virtues were
descending and ascending.

Look at the incarnate Son of God
and you will see
all the virtues for which you strive
in their perfection,
fully and completely at work.

He acted out in his own life
the way of salvation
so that all of us, whether great or small,
could learn from him
how to take the first step
on the path to virtue.

In him
we are able to find
the ultimate example
of the perfection to which we are called,

as we move one step at a time,
from the good to the better.

And as we practice these virtues,
the Son of God is made perfect
in our hearts.
The body of Christ
is made complete in us, his members,
who with a committed heart
and eagerness
live a life of good deeds
to which God gives wings.

All Through the Day

Perfection comes one step at a time.

My Day Is Ending

Spend a moment welcoming the dark.
Make friends with the silence of the night.

In your mind construct a ladder
that joins the floor and ceiling of this dark space.
Watch as a figure descends,
as it comes towards you and is absorbed, as it were,
into your own skin, into your own heart.
Make it welcome.
Borrow its courage and approach the ladder,
feeling a great weight but an eagerness to be about your climb.
Take a step at a time.
As you near the top, the weight seems less and less.
The steps seem easier.
It is almost as though you had wings.

Night Prayer

How precious to me is your steadfast love, O God!
I take refuge in the shadow of your wings
and feast on the abundance of your table.
I depend on the river of your gifts.
For with you is the fountain of life;
only in your light do I see light.
Amen.

Day Twenty-Six

My Day Begins

I saw
seven pillars
supporting a round dome of iron
and standing on top of this dome
I saw a singularly beautiful figure.

The figure is Wisdom
through whom all things
are created and ruled by God.
She was with God
before any of earth's and heaven's creatures
came to be.
She is God's great adornment
and the wide stairway to all the virtues
that are alive in him.

She protects and guides
everyone who seeks
to follow her,
and embraces with great love
those who are faithful to her.
She cannot be overthrown

by craftiness or mere power.

Her depths are hidden
in the heart of the father
and invisible to human eyes.
Her secrets are exposed and open to God alone.
For the majesty of God which she mirrors
is without beginning or end,
bright with incomparable glory
and so radiant that we cannot look directly upon it.

She will be with us
to the end of time,
unceasingly admonishing us
to follow where she leads.

All Through the Day

Follow where Wisdom leads.

My Day Is Ending

Spend a moment welcoming the dark.
Make friends with the silence of the night.

Grow accustomed to the dark,
opening and closing your eyes until bit by bit
a soft, undefined outline
of the space and its furnishings emerge.
Now at the edge of the space light a single candle,
actual or imagined, but real,
and watch as its glow spreads to every corner of the room.
Give it a name. Call it Wisdom.
And with your eyes trace a dimly lit
but certain path to its foot.
Hear yourself saying: "I will go where Wisdom leads."

Night Prayer

How precious to me is your steadfast love, O God!
I take refuge in the shadow of your wings
and feast on the abundance of your table.
I depend on the river of your gifts.
For with you is the fountain of life;
only in your light do I see light.
Amen.

Day Twenty-Seven

My Day Begins

I saw
sitting on a chair
a young man,
magnificent in his manhood,
who looked out on the world
crying out loudly. . . .

You have been given much.
Therefore much will be asked of you.
But in all things
the Son of Man is your helper.
Because heaven has chosen you,
he will answer
if you call on him.
If you knock at his door,
he will open it to you.
You have been given the gift of knowledge;
all that you need is within you.
But this being so,
God will examine you closely
and remember what he finds.

God requires of you, therefore,
a tender conscience,
a sensitive and repentant heart,
that will restrain you
when you feel
the almost suffocating attraction of sin.
The Son of Man will not let you out of his sight.
Call upon him,
and keep calling,
begging him to protect you
from the pull of the flesh
and the efforts of evil spirits.

He will do for you what you ask.

He will make his dwelling place with you.

All Through the Day

He will make his dwelling place with you.

My Day Is Ending

Spend a moment welcoming the dark.
Make friends with the silence of the night.

Across the room
is the young man of Hildegard's vision.
He is speaking:
"Much has been given to you,
but I have not stopped giving—if you will only ask."
Repeat his promise over and over again
until it is part of you,
until it drowns out the promises
that the world has made to you this day.
Let the silence return.
Then pray: "Come, make your dwelling place with me."

Night Prayer

How precious to me is your steadfast love, O God!
I take refuge in the shadow of your wings
and feast on the abundance of your table.
I depend on the river of your gifts.
For with you is the fountain of life;
only in your light do I see light.
Amen.

Day Twenty-Eight

My Day Begins

I saw
a wheel suspended in the air,
and in it was a person
visible only from the breast up,
looking with a piercing gaze
at the world.

Don't be foolish!

Lazily and shamefully
you shrink into yourself,
unwilling to open your eyes
to see how good your soul could be.

You cannot offer the excuse
that you lack any good thing
that would inspire you to love God.

You have the power to master yourself,
to refuse to revel in injustice.
You can run from illicit pleasure
and in the process,
by bearing his cross in your body,
honor the martyrdom

of God's incarnate Son.

God has given you the power
to do good and avoid evil.
And you will have to answer to him
for your knowledge of good and evil,
and your own humanity.
Too often you turn your back on good
and do evil.
Too often you choose to sin freely
rather than restrain yourself.

But you have no excuse.

All Through the Day

You lack nothing that you need.

My Day Is Ending

Spend a moment welcoming the dark.
Make friends with the silence of the night.

Close your eyes to all that is around you.
Now slowly open them.
At the far corner of the room
suspended in midair is the wheel of Hildegard's vision,
and within it the same figure
who chides you for your cowardice and laziness.

Open your eyes to what you are,
to what you have become.
Open them to what you could be.
With all you have been given,
why do you settle for so little?

Night Prayer

How precious to me is your steadfast love, O God!
I take refuge in the shadow of your wings
and feast on the abundance of your table.
I depend on the river of your gifts.
For with you is the fountain of life;
only in your light do I see light.
Amen.

Day Twenty-Nine

My Day Begins

*I saw
a white-winged figure
standing in a corner
whose face was so bright
that you could not look into it directly.*

God's generosity
flows out to those
who in open and simple faith,
in good and bad times alike,
support and expand
the building of the City of God,
watching and working
and doing all that must be done
for all within its walls.

They avoid
destructive, fatal hate and envy,
and the petty quarreling
of both the faithful and the faithless,
and cling to their vision of eternal peace.

These true believers

tire themselves out
doing good for others
working with a calm and bright vision
of what can be.

In so doing they touch God,
and as they seek to make perfect
the world around them
their souls are saved
and they come to a profound knowledge of him.

Building the City of God
is a living, lasting proof
that our soul has sought God.

All Through the Day

In serving others we touch God.

LET THERE BE LIGHT

My Day Is Ending

Spend a moment welcoming the dark.
Make friends with the silence of the night.

In the corner of the room is Hildegard's winged figure.
The darkness gives way to light.
The walls crumble
and the silence is broken by all the voices of your life . . .
your family, your friends, fellow workers,
strangers in the streets, the hungry, the homeless.
The room is full.
Everywhere you look are faces.
This is the City of God.

Reach out and touch its features.
You are touching the face of God.

Night Prayer

How precious to me is your steadfast love, O God!
I take refuge in the shadow of your wings
and feast on the abundance of your table.
I depend on the river of your gifts.
For with you is the fountain of life;
only in your light do I see light.
Amen.

Day Thirty

My Day Begins

I saw
the sun, the moon, and the stars,
sparkling in the sky like great ornaments,
but now at rest,
their orbit stilled.
No longer did they divide day from night.
Now there was no night, but only day.

The beloved John has written:
"And night shall be no more;
they need no light
of lamp or sun;
for the Lord God will be their light
and they shall reign for ever and ever."

Which is to say:
in the same way that
we sometimes hide our treasures
and at other times display them,
night hides the day,
and day dispels the darkness
to light up our days.
But this will change.
Time will be transformed;

night will be put to final flight,
and its darkness
will be no more.
We will no longer need to light our lamps.
The sun will not go down.
The day will be endless.
The Ruler of all,
in his changeless glory,
will illumine those
who have,
through his grace,
escaped the darkness.

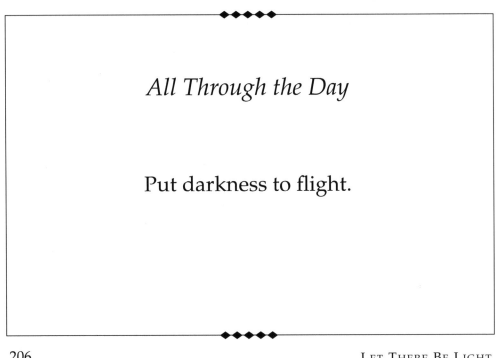

All Through the Day

Put darkness to flight.

My Day Is Ending

Spend a moment welcoming the dark.
Make friends with the silence of the night.

Now put it to flight.

With a single candle or bulb, or with a dozen,
lighted one by one,
imagine the end of time,
when darkness will no longer triumph even for a moment.
Then remind yourself
that it is not a matter of time
but of love,
of surrender,
to the changeless
unfaltering love of God.

Night Prayer

How precious to me is your steadfast love, O God!
I take refuge in the shadow of your wings
and feast on the abundance of your table.
I depend on the river of your gifts.
For with you is the fountain of life;
only in your light do I see light.
Amen.

One Final Word

In her best-known work, *Scivias,* Hildegard ends each of its three major series of visions with a version of the same invitation: "Let those who live with eyes wide open and hear with open ears welcome with love these mystical words, which have come from him who is Life."

This book has brought together just a few of those "words," arranged in the form of daily meditations in order to provide you an easily accessible gateway into the spiritual wisdom of this important spiritual guide . . . and a gateway opening on your own spiritual path.

You may decide that Hildegard of Bingen is someone whose visionary experience of God is one that you wish to explore more closely and deeply. In which case you should get a copy of one of the many full texts of her works that have become available in recent years and pray it as you have prayed this gateway journey.

You may decide that her experience has not helped you. There are many other teachers. Somewhere there is the right teacher for your own, very special, absolutely unique journey of the spirit. You will find your teacher, you will discover your path. We would not be searching, as St. Augustine reminds us, if we had not already been found.